My First Animal Library

Penguins

by Cari Meister

Ideas for Parents and Teachers

Bullfrog Books let children practice reading informational texts at the earliest reading levels. Repetition, familiar words, and photo labels support early readers.

Before Reading

- Discuss the cover photo. What does it tell them?

- Look at the picture glossary together. Read and discuss the words.

Read the Book

- "Walk" through the book and look at the photos. Let the child ask questions. Point out the photo labels.

- Read the book to the child, or have him or her read independently.

After Reading

- Prompt the child to think more. Ask: Why do you think penguins are black and white? How is a penguin like other birds? How is it different?

Bullfrog Books are published by Jump!
5357 Penn Avenue South
Minneapolis, MN 55419
www.jumplibrary.com

Library of Congress Cataloging-in-Publication Data

Meister, Cari.
  Penguins / by Cari Meister.
     p. cm. -- (Bullfrog books. My first animal library, zoo animals)
  Summary: "This easy-to-read nonfiction book tells a story about how penguins are adapted to swim in cold water and how they survive in the wild"-- Provided by publisher.
  Audience: 005.
  Audience: K to grade 3.
  Includes bibliographical references and index.
  ISBN 978-1-62031-066-3 (hardcover) -- ISBN 978-1-62496-066-6 (ebook)
  1. Penguins--Juvenile literature. I. Title.
  QL696.S47M45 2014
  598.47--dc23
                                             2013006900

Series Editor: Rebecca Glaser
Series Designer: Ellen Huber
Book Designer: Danny Nanos

Photo Credits: All photos by Shutterstock except the following: Alamy 16-17, 23tr; Getty 14

Printed in the United States at Corporate Graphics in North Mankato, Minnesota.

5-2013 / PO 1003
10 9 8 7 6 5 4 3 2 1

Table of Contents

Swimming Birds

A penguin is a bird.

It has feathers.

It lays eggs.

But it cannot fly.

That's okay.

It can waddle.

It can swim.

It can slide on its belly.

Wheee!

Splash!

A penguin jumps into the cold water.

He swims.

His body is made
for swimming.

Its sleek shape
moves fast.

13

His thick wings are flippers.

flipper

They paddle.
They steer.

15

What's this?

A school of krill.
Yum!

She grabs some
with her
sharp beak.

krill

chick

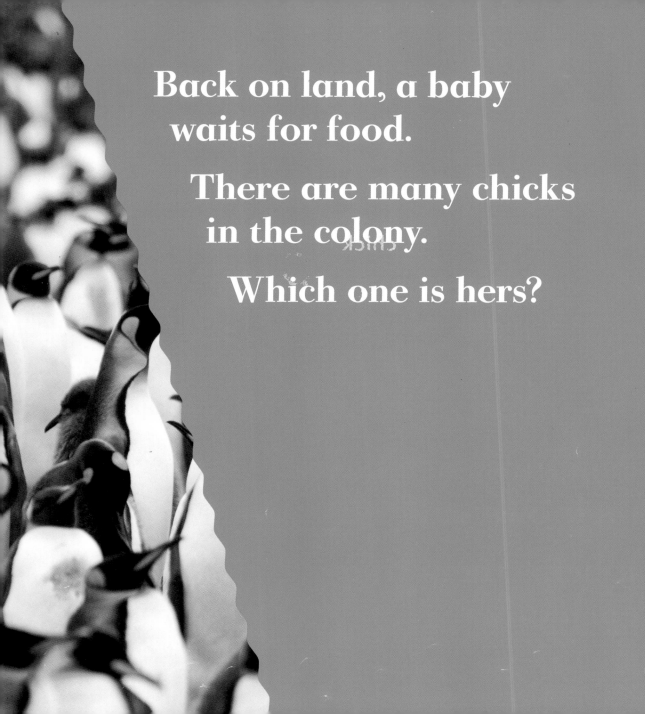

Back on land, a baby
waits for food.

There are many chicks
in the colony.

Which one is hers?

Penguins each have their own call.

It helps them find each other.

Hi, Mama!

Parts of a Penguin

bill
The sharp outer mouth part that helps a penguin grab fish.

eyes
Penguins can see at night and during the day.

feathers
Like all birds, penguins have feathers that keep them warm.

webbed feet
Penguins have webbed feet that help them paddle in the water.

Picture Glossary

chick
A baby penguin.

krill
Small fish that look like shrimp.

colony
A large group of birds that live together.

sleek
Having a streamlined shape that moves easily through water.

flippers
Flat, thick wings that help a penguin swim.

waddle
To walk with short steps, swaying side to side.

Index

To Learn More

Learning more is as easy as 1, 2, 3.

1) Go to www.factsurfer.com

2) Enter "penguins" into the search box.

3) Click the "Surf" button to see a list of websites.

With factsurfer.com, finding more information is just a click away.